Cambridge **Discovery Education**™

▶ **INTERACTIVE READERS**

Series editor: Bob Hastings

WONDERS OF THE WORLD

A1+

Nic Harris

CAMBRIDGE
UNIVERSITY PRESS

32 Avenue of the Americas, New York, NY 10013-2473, USA

Cambridge University Press is part of the University of Cambridge.

It furthers the University's mission by disseminating knowledge in the pursuit of education, learning and research at the highest international levels of excellence.

www.cambridge.org
Information on this title: www.cambridge.org/9781107642980

First published 2014
5th printing 2016

Printed in Dubai by Oriental Press

A catalogue record for this publication is available from the British Library.

Library of Congress Cataloguing in Publication data
Harris, Nicholas.
  Wonders of the world / Nic Harris.
    pages cm. -- (Cambridge discovery interactive readers)
  ISBN 978-1-107-64298-0 (pbk. : alk. paper)
  1. Seven Wonders of the World--Juvenile literature. 2. English language--Textbooks for foreign speakers. 3. Readers (Elementary) I. Title.

N5333.H27 2013
031.02--dc23

                    2013025131

ISBN 978-1-107-64298-0

Additional resources for this publication at www.cambridge.org

Layout services, art direction, book design, and photo research: Q2ABillSMITH GROUP
Editorial services: Hyphen S.A.
Audio production: CityVox, New York
Video production: Q2ABillSMITH GROUP

Contents

Before You Read:
Get Ready!

Wonders: the oldest, the most beautiful, and the most interesting things in the world.

Words to Know

Look at the pictures. Then complete the sentences below with the correct words.

building

earthquake

list

mountain

statue

stones

1. People often make a _____ of the things they want to buy at a shop.

2. People live and work in this _____ .

3. Everest is the highest _____ in the world.

4. When people need to build very strong things like houses, they often use _____ .

5. In front of the art museum, there is a very big, beautiful _____ of horses running.

6. An _____ is a very bad thing. When one happens, many people can die.

Read the text. Then complete the sentences below with the correct highlighted words.

In the world, there are many ancient buildings and statues. People made them a long time ago. Sometimes we can see them today because they are above the ground. But other times we cannot see them because they are below the ground. Some old buildings are still standing. We can see them well. But others fall down and we can only see parts of them. Some of these old buildings were temples. People came to these places to talk to their gods. They asked their gods to help them and to make their lives better.

1 We walk on the _____ .

2 _____ buildings are very old.

3 When people wanted help, they sometimes asked their _____ to make things better.

4 When the wind is strong, trees can _____ .

5 _____ are buildings that people make for their religion. People come there, but they don't live there.

CHAPTER 1

The World's Ancient Wonders

WE SEE LISTS ON THE INTERNET ALL THE TIME: TEN BEST MOVIES, BOOKS, VACATION PLACES . . . BUT MAKING LISTS ISN'T NEW.

Around 140 BCE, a Greek man, Antipater of Sidon, made a list of the Seven **Wonders** of the World. Most were beautiful buildings or statues in or near Greece. Only one is still standing today. Go online to learn more.

The Colossus of Rhodes: a 30-meter-high statue of a god. It only stood for 56 years before it fell down in an earthquake.

The Hanging Gardens of Babylon: A king called Nebuchadnezzar II built these beautiful gardens for his wife.

The Statue of Zeus: a 12-meter-high statue of the Greek god Zeus.

The Mausoleum of Halicarnassus: When a ruler[1] called Mausolus died, they put his body here. Now buildings for dead people are called mausoleums.

The Lighthouse at Alexandria: a 120-meter-tall building to help ships find the land. It also fell down in a big earthquake.

The Temple of Artemis: Antipater's favorite wonder. There are only a few stones today to show us where it was.

The Great Pyramid: the oldest of the **ancient** wonders and the only one that is still standing. For 3,800 years, it was the tallest building in the world.

....
[1]**ruler:** a very important person who tells people what to do

? **EVALUATE**
Which two of these ancient wonders would you like to travel to the past to see?

The Lighthouse at Alexandria helped ships to travel safely.

CHAPTER 2

Bernard Weber, the man behind it all

The New 7 Wonders of the World

ON THE SEVENTH DAY OF THE SEVENTH MONTH OF THE YEAR 2007, THE NEW7WONDERS FOUNDATION NAMED SEVEN NEW WONDERS.

In 2001, Bernard Weber, a Canadian, started the New7Wonders Foundation. He wanted people to know more about the beautiful cities, buildings, and statues in the world. He wanted people to understand how they are important to our history.

Weber asked people in every country to vote[2] for their favorite man-made wonder. After everybody voted, there were 77 wonders on the list. A group of experts[3] chose 21 of these. Then, people voted again online and on the phone. Here are the seven new wonders they chose.

[2] **vote:** choose something from a list

[3] **expert:** someone who knows a lot about something

Petra (Jordan)

The Western world knew nothing of this ancient city until 1812. Then Johann Burckhardt from Switzerland discovered[4] it. The Nabataean people built the city between 300 BCE and 100 CE. Many cities are built near mountains, but Petra is *inside* a mountain!

Petra is sometimes called "the rose red city" because of its colors. It was a very important market town – people bought and sold things there. Today, you can see only about 15 percent of the city. The other 85 percent is under the ground.

If you want to see Petra, watch the movie *Indiana Jones and the Last Crusade*. The end of the movie is in Petra.

....

[4]**discover:** find something

The Al Khazneh temple at Petra

The stone of the monument changes color at different times of day – from pink to white to yellow.

The Taj Mahal (India)

Emperor[5] Shah Jahan loved his wife very much. She died in 1631, after she had her fourteenth child. The emperor was so sad that he wanted to build a beautiful temple for her. The next year, work started on the Taj Mahal.

About 20,000 men and 1,000 elephants worked for 22 years to build it. A story at the time said that the emperor cut off the hands of the workers when it was finished. He didn't want them to make another **monument** as beautiful as the Taj Mahal.

[5]**emperor:** the leader of a very large group of people and countries

Video Quest

Taj Mahal

Watch this video to learn more about temples in India. Why is the Jama Masjid famous?

The Great Wall of China

Emperor Qin Shi Huang lived in China in the 3rd **century** BCE. He was worried about some unfriendly countries, so he built a wall to stop other people from coming into China. Later, between 1368 and 1644, the Ming Emperors made the wall longer. In the end, it was 8,851 kilometers long.

It was very hard, **dangerous** work to make the wall. More than one million people died from the cold or because they didn't have enough food.

For many years people stole stones from the wall to make their own houses. So today, only some parts of the wall are standing.

Some parts of the Great Wall of China are in the mountains.

11

The Colosseum (Italy)

Work began on this building in 72 CE, in the time of the Roman Emperor Vespasian. At one time, 50,000 people came to the Colosseum to watch sports and games. But these weren't the sports we enjoy today. They were fights[6] with men called gladiators or with dangerous animals. Thousands of people died.

After a long time these games stopped. Then, between the 6th and 12th centuries, the Colosseum was a place for shops and houses. A large part of the building fell down in an earthquake in 1349, but you can still go to Rome and visit it today.

[6]**fight:** when two or more people hit each other

Gladiators fighting in the Colosseum

The mountain city of Machu Picchu

Machu Picchu (Peru)

This is called "The City in the Clouds." Around 1450, the Incas started to build Machu Picchu, a beautiful city between two mountains, 2,500 meters above the **sea**.

The city was small. About 750 people lived here, and there were only 200 buildings. No one knows why the Incas built it. Maybe it was a vacation place for an important man called Pachacuti.

In the early 1500s, the Spanish came to South America and destroyed[7] many Inca cities. But they did not find Machu Picchu. It was a lost city until American Hiram Bingham discovered it again in 1911. Now lots of **tourists** visit it.

....
[7]**destroy:** do something bad to a thing or place so nobody can use it again

Chichén Itzá (Mexico)

The Mayans built a city in Chichén Itzá because there was water under the ground for their farms. They began to build it in the 6th century CE, but about 1200, they left. Nobody is sure why. When the Spanish arrived in the 15th century, the city was empty.

El Castillo, or the temple of Kukulcán, is the most famous building in Chichén Itzá. Kukulcán was a Mayan god. He was half bird, half snake. Twice a year, the light from the sun does something **strange** on the walls of El Castillo. You can see a snake moving from the top to the bottom.

Video Quest

Mayan Wonder

Watch the video to learn more about Chichén Itzá. Where did the Mayans play sports?

People came to El Castillo to talk to their god, Kukulcán.

Christ the Reedemer looks out at Rio de Janeiro.

DID YOU KNOW...?

The New7Wonders Foundation didn't forget about one of the ancient wonders. Number 8 on their list is the Great Pyramid of Giza.

Christ the Redeemer Statue (Brazil)

At 30 meters tall, this statue is one of the tallest in the world. It's on the top of Corcovado Mountain. Workers used stone from Sweden. They finished it in 1931.

In 2008, lightning[8] hit the statue on the head and fingers. Then, in 2010, some people painted the statue's head and arms and wrote words on the face. But don't worry. The statue is still standing, and now it's clean again.

[8]**lightning:** light in the sky in a storm. It is sometimes dangerous.

The waterfalls at Iguazu

CHAPTER 3

Other Wonders

THERE ARE MANY DIFFERENT KINDS OF WONDERS IN OUR WORLD.

In 2011, the New7Wonders Foundation named the New 7 Wonders of **Nature**.

Amazon Rainforest (South America): This rainforest[9] is the largest rainforest in the world. About 60 percent of it is in Brazil, and other parts are in seven other South American countries. The Amazon River goes through the middle of it.

Iguazu Falls (between Brazil and Argentina): In some places the waterfalls are 82 meters high. Between November and March, about 13,000 cubic meters of water per second fall into the river below.

[9]**rainforest:** a place that has a lot of trees and is hot and wet

Table Mountain (South Africa): This 1,100-meter-high mountain is near the city of Cape Town.

Jeju Island (South Korea): Many tourists visit this beautiful island to see its beaches, parks, and the famous *dol hareubang*, stone statues of old men.

One of the dol hareubang

Komodo (Indonesia): This island is famous because of the Komodo dragon. This animal can be 3 meters long and 70 kilograms. It has big teeth and can be dangerous.

Ha Long Bay (Vietnam): There are 1,600 islands here. There are no people on most of them.

A Komodo dragon

Puerto Princesa Undergound River (Philippines): This 8.2-kilometer river runs under the St. Paul Mountains and into the South China Sea.

These seven places came from a list of 28 possible wonders. It was hard to choose just seven. Some of the ones that did not make the list are Mount Everest, the Grand Canyon, and the Northern Lights.

Video Quest

The Northern Lights

Watch this video to see the Northern Lights. How old are the Northern Lights? Do you think they should be on the list?

In 2003, BBC Television made this list of the Seven Wonders of the Industrial[10] World.

The *Great Eastern:* This was the biggest ship in the world in 1858. It could carry 4,000 people around the world without stopping.

The Bell Rock Lighthouse: Workers built this in the sea, 18 kilometers from Scotland.

Brooklyn Bridge: This 1,825-meter-long bridge connects two parts of New York City: Manhattan and Brooklyn.

The London Sewage System: This underground system takes dirty water out of the city of London.

[10] **industrial:** a name for the many things people make in factories and businesses

Thousands of people use the Brooklyn Bridge every day.

The First Transcontinental Railroad: This railroad in the USA was made in 1869. For the first time, trains could travel the 2,858 kilometers from the east all the way to California.

The Panama Canal: This man-made river goes from the Caribbean Sea to the Pacific Ocean. Before the Canal, ships had to travel 15,000 kilometers around South America.

The Hoover Dam: Engineers finished this enormous[11] dam in 1936, in the USA. They named it after the American president at that time, Herbert Hoover.

There are many more lists, too. For example, there is a list of the seven most fantastic cities in the world. Is your city one of them? Go online to find out.

....
[11]**enormous:** very, very big

The Hoover Dam has thousands of liters of water behind it and in front of it.

?

EVALUATE

You have to choose two Wonders of the Industrial World. Which two do you think made people's lives easier and safer?

LANCASTER-6
BIRD-IN-HAND
NAMED FOR
A PICTURE ON OLD HOTEL'S
SWINGING SIGN
FOUNDED
1734

CHAPTER 4

What Do You Think?

PEOPLE MAKE SOME STRANGE LISTS.

For example, The Seven Funniest Names for Towns. On this list are towns like Boring (USA), Why (USA), and Box (UK). Or The Seven Worst Things You Can Eat. Why do you think people make these lists?

Here are some lists for *you* to make.

Interesting Places

Write down some interesting places to see in your country. They could be monuments, buildings, natural places, or cities. Then choose seven and say why you chose them.

Movies

Did you see any of these movies: *Star Wars, The Matrix, The Lord of the Rings*? People voted for these on a list of their hundred favorite movies. Make a list of your top seven movies. Say why you like them so much.

Favorite Things

Think about this. Tomorrow, you are going to lose everything you have. Well, almost everything. You can keep only seven things. Write a list of your seven favorite things, and say why you want to keep them.

Places in this Book

Choose seven places from this book that you would really like to see. Why did you choose them?

After You Read

Choose the Correct Answers

Choose (A), (B), or (C) to correctly complete the sentences.

1 The Colossus of Rhodes _____ .

  (A) was the oldest of the ancient wonders

  (B) was a statue of a man and a tiger

  (C) didn't stand for very many years

2 Petra was an important city because _____ .

  (A) it was near a big river

  (B) people did business there

  (C) it was on top of a mountain

3 The wife of the Indian emperor Shah Jahan died _____ .

  (A) because she was old

  (B) after she had a child

  (C) in a fight with her sister

4 From the 1st to the 5th century CE, people came to the Colosseum to _____ .

  (A) buy and sell food and other things

  (B) watch gladiators and animals fight

  (C) talk to their gods and goddesses

5 When the Spanish came to Peru, they _____ .

  (A) lived and worked in Machu Picchu

  (B) found Machu Picchu and destroyed it

  (C) didn't know anything about Machu Picchu

6 The Mayan god Kukulcán _____ .

  (A) didn't have the body of a person

  (B) often ate animals like birds and snakes

  (C) lived under the city of Chichén Itzá

7 Water from the Iguazu Falls goes _____ .

(A) into the sea

(B) under the ground

(C) into a river

8 The London Sewage System _____ .

(A) makes the city a cleaner place

(B) is a railroad under the ground

(C) is something people walk across

Complete the Text

Use the words in the box to complete the story about another wonder of the world.

god	ground	list	stones	temple

The New7Wonders Foundation made a **1** _____ of 21 wonders of the world. One of these was Stonehenge in the UK. People called Druids built it between 3000 and 1600 BCE. It was a kind of **2** _____ where the Druids met. These people didn't have one **3** _____ , they had many: one for the sun, the rain, the wind, etc. They talked to all of them. Stonehenge was not a building with walls. It was a group of 30 big, heavy **4** _____ . Today only 17 of these are standing. The others fell down and are now on the **5** _____ .

My Opinion

Complete the sentences with places from this book.

_____ is the most beautiful man-made place.

_____ is the most beautiful natural place.

_____ is the most interesting place.

_____ is not a very interesting place to me.

_____ is a dangerous place.

Answer Key

Words to Know, page 4

1 list **2** building **3** mountain **4** stones **5** statue
6 earthquake

Words to Know, page 5

1 ground **2** Ancient **3** gods **4** fall down **5** temples

Evaluate, page 7

Answers will vary.

Video Quest, page 11

There are statues in the Indian temples. The Jama Masjid is the largest mosque in India.

Video Quest, page 14

The Mayans played sports in the ball court building.

Video Quest, page 17

The Northern Lights are billions of years old.

Evaluate, page 19

Answers will vary.

Choose the Correct Answers, page 22

1 C **2** B **3** B **4** B **5** C **6** A **7** C **8** A

Complete the Text, page 23

1 list **2** temple **3** god **4** stones **5** ground

My Opinion, page 23

Answers will vary.